By Jim Gigliotti

Consultant: Craig Ellenport
Former Senior Editor
NFL.com

BEARPORT
PUBLISHING

New York, New York

Credits

Cover, © AP Photo/Paul Spinelli; Title Page, © Ed Ruvalcaba/Image of Sport/Newscom; 4, © AP Photo/Paul Spinelli; 5, © AP Photo/Paul Spinelli; 6, © David Eulitt/The Kansas City Star/Newscom; 7, © Joe Robbins; 9, © Gary Cosby; 10, Courtesy Rivers of Hope Foundation; 11, © Sean Meyers/Icon SMI/Newscom; 12, © Sean Meyers/Icon SMI/Newscom; 13, © Tom Walkon/Icon Sportswire/Newscom; 14, © K.C. Alfred/ZumaPress/Newscom; 15, © AP Photo/Denis Poroy; 16, © Liz Leyden/istock; 17, © Archie Carpenter/UPI/Newscom; 18, © K.C. Alfred/Zuma Press/Newscom; 19, © Archie Carpenter/UPI/Newscom; 20, © Kevin Dietsch/UPI/Newscom; 20, © Paul Buck/EPA/Newscom; 22, © Ed Ruvalcaba/Image of Sport/Newscom.

Publisher: Kenn Goin
Senior Editor: Joyce Tavolacci
Creative Director: Spencer Brinker
Production and Photo Research: Shoreline Publishing Group LLC
Series Design: Dawn Beard Creative

Library of Congress Cataloging-in-Publication Data

Names: Gigliotti, Jim.
Title: Philip Rivers / by Jim Gigliotti.
Description: New York, New York : Bearport Publishing, [2016] | Series:
  Football heroes making a difference | Includes bibliographical references
  and index.
Identifiers: LCCN 2015033443 | ISBN 9781943553419 (library binding) | ISBN
  1943553416 (library binding)
Subjects: LCSH: Rivers, Philip, 1981-—Juvenile literature. | Football
  players—United States—Biography—Juvenile literature. | Quarterbacks
  (Football)—United States—Biography—Juvenile literature. | Football
  players—United States—Conduct of life—Juvenile literature.
Classification: LCC GV939.R56 G54 2016 | DDC 796.332092—dc23
LC record available at http://lccn.loc.gov/2015033443

For more information, write to Bearport Publishing Company, Inc., 45 West 21st Street, Suite 3B, New York, New York 10010. Printed in the United States of America.

10 9 8 7 6 5 4 3 2 1

CONTENTS

Last-Minute Victory

It was November 30, 2014, and the San Diego Chargers were facing the Baltimore Ravens. The Ravens led 33–27. Just 41 seconds remained in the game. The Chargers had **possession** of the ball at the one-yard (0.9 m) line. For Chargers quarterback Philip Rivers, it was now or never.

Philip called a play in the **huddle**. Because he had studied Baltimore's **defense**, he knew the play would work. He took the **snap**, dropped back two quick steps, and tossed the ball to **wide receiver** Eddie Royal. Eddie darted into the **end zone**. Touchdown, San Diego! Moments later, Nick Novak kicked the extra point. The Chargers won the game 34–33!

Chargers receivers Keenan Allen (#13) and Eddie Royal celebrate the touchdown!

Philip (#17) calls out a play to his team before a snap.

Philip passed for 383 yards (350 m) during the game against Baltimore. He holds the Chargers' single-game passing record of 503 yards (460 m), set against Green Bay in 2015.

Never Give Up

Philip is at his best when the Chargers need him the most. The 2014 win against the Ravens marked the nineteenth time in Philip's career that he led the Chargers to a comeback victory. He's especially good at turning things around for his team during the final seconds of a game. For example, in a 2013 game against the Kansas City Chiefs, Philip's last pass was a 26-yard (24 m) strike to wide receiver Seyi Ajirotutu. There were only 24 seconds left in the game. Seyi caught the pass and San Diego won 41–38! Philip's ability to perform under pressure and his never-give-up attitude have made him a fan favorite.

Seyi Ajirotutu (#18) caught Philip's pass for the game-winning touchdown.

Philip's blockers protect
him as he hurls the ball.

During the 2006 season, Philip guided
the Chargers to back-to-back wins in
two games in which his team trailed
by at least 17 points. He was the first
NFL quarterback ever to do this.

A Coach's Son

Philip grew up in Decatur, Alabama. His mom was a teacher, and his dad was a high school football coach. Philip's parents taught him the importance of family, education, and helping others. They also shared their love of football with their son. As a child, Philip was a **ball boy** at his dad's games at Decatur High School. He couldn't wait until he was old enough to play football on his dad's team.

In 1996, when Philip was a freshman in high school, his dad became the head coach at nearby Athens High School. Philip joined the team. He played **linebacker** because the team already had a quarterback. Even though Philip made a good linebacker, he wasn't happy in that position. In 1998, Philip's dream came true when he became the team's **starting** quarterback.

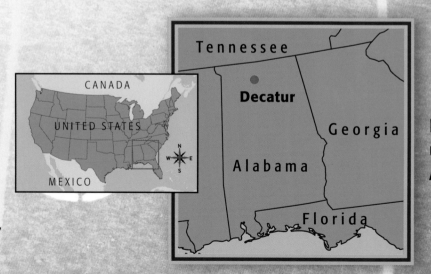

Philip grew up in northern Alabama.

Philip (right) with his dad at an Athens High School game

When Philip was a boy, his teacher asked him to show the class what he wanted to be when he grew up. Philip pasted a photo of himself on the cover of *Sports Illustrated* magazine.

Wolfpack Quarterback

In addition to being a star athlete, Philip was a great student. He worked hard and finished high school early. A lot of colleges with strong football teams were interested in Philip. Some schools thought he would make a good linebacker, or perhaps a **safety**, but Philip wanted to keep playing quarterback. He decided to attend North Carolina State, where the Wolfpack's coach would give Philip a chance to play the position he loved.

In the fall of 2000, Philip became North Carolina State's starting quarterback. He went on to start all 51 of the Wolfpack's games during his four seasons there, from 2000 through 2003.

Because Philip started college early, he wasn't around to take his high school sweetheart, Tiffany, to the senior prom. However, the two stayed in touch and married in 2001.

Philip gets ready to pass the ball as the Wolfpack's quarterback.

Ready for the NFL

Philip turned out to be the best quarterback North Carolina State had ever had. After graduating in 2003, Philip was ready for the NFL **Draft**. "Whichever team I go to will be getting a guy who's passionate, dependable, and who hates to lose," he said.

In 2004, the New York Giants picked Philip as the fourth overall choice of the draft. The same day, the Giants traded him to the San Diego Chargers. The Chargers already had a good quarterback in Drew Brees, but they felt that Philip could be their next big star.

For two years, Philip learned all he could from watching Drew Brees play. In 2006, Philip became the Chargers' starting quarterback— and has been a superstar on the field ever since.

North Carolina State stopped using Philip's jersey number when he graduated.

Philip (#17) hands off the ball to a running back.

In 2006, Philip's first season as San Diego's starting quarterback, the Chargers set a team record for wins. That year, they won 14 games, losing only 2 games.

Military Thanks

Philip quickly settled into his role as a leader on the football field. He also became a leader in the community. San Diego is home to many people who serve in the U.S. military. To thank them for their service, the Chargers hold a practice at a local military base each year. In 2013, the team visited the aircraft carrier the *USS Ronald Reagan.*

During practice, Philip and his teammates ran plays on the deck of the huge ship. Then Philip signed autographs for the service members and their families. "This is a small way of giving back and showing our appreciation for what they do," Philip said.

Philip signs footballs for members of the U.S. military.

Philip (in red) and the Chargers practicing on an aircraft carrier

One of the largest fleets of U.S. Navy ships in the world is in San Diego.

Helping Kids

Philip has never forgotten what his parents taught him about helping others and dedicates his time to helping children in need. In the spring of 2014, Philip learned about a very sick two-year-old boy named Stephen from a local newspaper reporter. Philip wanted to help the boy. That's how he discovered the Ronald McDonald House **Charities**. The group gives families a free place to stay while their sick children are being treated in the hospital. The reporter told Philip he was going to **donate** $1 to the Ronald McDonald House for every passing yard Philip made that season.

Philip loved the idea and encouraged other people to donate. Philip passed for 4,286 yards (3,919 m) that season. That's a lot of yards—and thousands of dollars raised for the Ronald McDonald House Charities!

A Ronald McDonald House

Philip has passed for more yards and touchdowns that any other quarterback in the Chargers' history!

Role Model

Philip will stop at nothing to make a child's dreams come true. One day, he got a call from an organization called the Make-A-Wish Foundation. A **critically** ill boy at a children's hospital in Los Angeles wanted more than anything to meet Philip. The very next day, Philip drove from San Diego to Los Angeles to play catch and watch football with the boy in his hospital room. "This seven-year-old could make any wish, and he wants to hang out with me," Philip said. "Man, you don't turn that one down."

Philip believes that athletes are role models for children—and he wants to be the best role model he can be. "There's more to being a professional athlete than what happens between the lines [on the field]," he says.

Gunner Rivers, one of Philip's children, joined him on the field after a game.

Philip and his wife Tiffany have five girls and two boys. "Win or lose, those seven children and my wife love me for being Dad and husband," Philip says.

Best of the Bunch

The San Diego Chargers have had a lot of great quarterbacks. However, Philip stands out as one of the best. He has broken many of the team's passing records, and he has also led the Chargers to the **playoffs** five times. All that's missing is a **Super Bowl** win. "We haven't accomplished the ultimate goal," Philip says. A Super Bowl win would be nice. However, as he says, "It's not about what I can do as an athlete. It's about what we can do as a community."

Philip does a lot to help the community. In 2011, he was one of three finalists for the Walter Payton NFL Man of the Year Award. The award honors a player for his excellence on the field and community involvement off the field. That combination makes Philip a true football hero.

Philip (left) and his fellow Walter Payton Award finalists, Charles Tillman and Matt Birk

20

Philip has won more games than any other Chargers starting quarterback in the team's history.

Philip set a Chargers record when he passed for 34 touchdowns in 2008. The previous record of 33, made by Dan Fouts in 1981, lasted 27 years.

The Philip File

Philip is a football hero on and off the field. Here are some highlights.

🏈 Ever since high school, Philip has worn a jersey with the number 17 on it. It's in honor of his dad, who also wore the number 17 when he was a player in high school.

🏈 With Philip leading the way, the Chargers have won the AFC West division championship every season, from 2006 through 2009.

🏈 Philip led all NFL quarterbacks when he passed for a career best of 4,710 yards (4,307 m) during the 2010 season.

🏈 Philip can sometimes be found playing catch with his kids at the Chargers' Qualcomm Stadium in San Diego.

Glossary

ball boy (BALL BOI) a child who retrieves balls during a football game

charities (CHA-ruh-teez) groups that help people in need

critically (KRIT-uh-kuhl-ee) seriously

defense (DEE-fens) players who have the job of stopping the other team from scoring

donate (DOH-nayt) to give something as a gift

draft (DRAFT) an event in which professional teams take turns choosing college athletes to play for them

end zone (END zohn) the area at either end of a football field where touchdowns are scored

huddle (HUD-ul) when the team groups together to hear a play being called

linebacker (LINE-bak-ur) a defensive player, on the second line of defenders, who makes tackles and defends passes

NFL (EN-EF-EL) letters standing for *National Football League*

playoffs (PLAY-awfss) a series of games played after the regular schedule to determine a champion

possession (poh-ZESH-uhn) when a team has the ball and is trying to score

safety (SAYF-tee) a defensive player who usually lines up farther back than other defensive players

snap (SNAP) the exchange of the ball from one player to another to begin each play

starting (START-ing) playing at the start of a game; the best player in a position

Super Bowl (SOO-pur BOHL) the NFL's championship game

wide receiver (WIDE ree-SEE-vur) a player whose job it is to catch passes

Bibliography

Acee, Kevin. "Helping Kids, Families With Some Passes." *The San Diego Union-Tribune* (April 28, 2014).

Bair, Scott. "Chargers: Rivers Embraces His Charity Work." *The San Diego Union-Tribune* (February 1, 2012).

Read More

Allen, Kathy. *Drew Brees (Football Stars Up Close)*. New York: Bearport (2013).

Stewart, Mark. *The San Diego Chargers (Team Spirit)*. Chicago: Norwood House Press (2008).

Whiting, Jim. *NFL Today: The Story of the San Diego Chargers*. Mankato, MN: Creative Paperbacks (2013).

Learn More Online

To learn more about Philip Rivers, visit
www.bearportpublishing.com/FootballHeroes

Index